Turn and Live

SERIES EDITORS
Joel R. Beeke & Jay T. Collier

Interest in the Puritans continues to grow, but many people find the reading of these giants of the faith a bit unnerving. This series seeks to overcome that barrier by presenting Puritan books that are convenient in size and unintimidating in length. Each book is carefully edited with modern readers in mind, smoothing out difficult language of a bygone era while retaining the meaning of the original authors. Books for the series are thoughtfully selected to provide some of the best counsel on important subjects that people continue to wrestle with today.

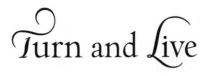

Turn and Live

Nathaniel Vincent

Edited by
Jonathon D. Beeke

Reformation Heritage Books
Grand Rapids, Michigan

Turn and Live
© 2015 by Reformation Heritage Books

Reformation Heritage Books
2965 Leonard St. NE
Grand Rapids, MI 49525
616-977-0889 / Fax 616-285-3246
orders@heritagebooks.org
www.heritagebooks.org

Originally published as *The Conversion of a Sinner Explained and Applied* (London, 1669).

Printed in the United States of America
15 16 17 18 19 20/10 9 8 7 6 5 4 3 2 1

Library of Congress Cataloging-in-Publication Data

Names: Vincent, Nathanael, 1639?-1697 author. | Beeke, Jonathon D., editor.
Title: Turn and live / Nathaniel Vincent ; edited by Jonathon D. Beeke.
Other titles: Conversion of a sinner explained and applied
Description: Grand Rapids, Michigan : Reformation Heritage Books, 2015. | Series: Puritan treasures for today | Originally published under title: The conversion of a sinner explained and applied : London : Printed for Tho. Parkhurst, 1669.
Identifiers: LCCN 2015041205 (print) | LCCN 2015042142 (ebook) | ISBN 9781601784353 (pbk. : alk. paper) | ISBN 9781601784360 (epub)
Subjects: LCSH: Conversion—Biblical teaching. | Bible. Ezekiel, XXXIII, 11—Criticism, interpretation, etc.
Classification: LCC BS1545.6.C59 V56 2015 (print) | LCC BS1545.6.C59 (ebook) | DDC 243—dc23
LC record available at http://lccn.loc.gov/2015041205

For additional Reformed literature, request a free book list from Reformation Heritage Books at the above regular or e-mail address.

Table of Contents

Preface

One of the earliest lessons a parent must teach his or her child is to come when called. Of course, obeying this call involves a physical response from the child; the child must, upon hearing the parent's directive, turn from whatever occupies his or her attention and go to the parent. As every parent has learned, however, the desired response is not always the outcome. It is, I presume, easy to imagine an energetic young boy running after a ball just outside his grasp, and he hears his father calling him to come back. Further, it is easy to imagine that the boy's energies are so focused on the ball that he chooses to ignore his father and continues in his chase of the runaway ball. And yet, because of his fixation on the ball, the boy does not realize that he is rushing out onto a busy and dangerous street; the father, on the other hand, is aware of the danger and anxiously calls his son to turn back out of concern for the boy's safety.

This simple analogy parallels what you will read in the following pages in several aspects: just as the father urgently calls out to his boy to stop his dangerous pursuit, so too God the Father graciously calls His creatures to turn from their dangerous pursuit of evil. In contrast, just as the boy recklessly chases an invaluable object and so places himself in danger, the sinner runs after the "shiny objects" of this world—material, temporal possessions or positions that will fade away—only to put himself under the very real threat and curse of the law: eternal death. Further, just as the running boy must stop, turn around, and even run from the imminent threat of the busy street, so too the sinner must stop, turn, and live.

God's call to the sinner to turn and live is serious and demands a response. This small book contains a sermon preached by Nathaniel Vincent (1638–1697) concerning this solemn subject. The original sermon, first published in 1669, was titled *The Conversion of a Sinner: Explained and Applied From Ezekiel 33:11, "Turn ye, turn ye, from your evil ways; for why will ye die, O house of Israel?"* As evident from the title, Vincent's text was this profound verse wherein God calls sinners to repentance. In a very clear, compelling, and passionate way, Vincent outlines the foolishness of continuing in the pathway of evil, the stubborn disposition of natural man to continue in this way, the gracious and repeated call of God to turn, and the wonderful remedy found in Christ. In typical Puritan fashion, Vincent also draws out several applications, or uses, of this doctrine.

While *Turn and Live* closely follows the content and structure of Vincent's original sermon, multiple edits and revisions have been made by the editor with the intent of making this sermon more readable and accessible. My desire is that upon taking up and reading *Turn and Live*, you may hear God's call to repent and believe in Him, a call that is repeated throughout the Old and New Testaments and here echoed by Vincent. While you yet have physical life, a simple choice remains: death or life. Pray God that He would raise you up by His Spirit from your dead state to live in Christ!

—Jonathon D. Beeke

CHAPTER 1

God's Call to Turn

Turn ye, turn ye, from your evil ways; for why will ye die, O house of Israel?
—Ezekiel 33:11

It is not easy to discern whether man displayed greater foolishness in departing from God at first, or whether his folly is now more inexcusable in refusing to return to Him. At first, Adam knew by blessed experience how good it was to be near his Maker, to enjoy the light of His countenance in the state of innocence; and yet Adam turned his back on God and decided to depart from his Creator. As a result, mankind now feels the effects of this apostasy, for he experiences various miseries, calamities, and vexations; and yet how difficult it is to persuade him to come back again to God! How easily are people induced to yield to Satan, desiring, as it were, to give themselves into the hands of a murderer. But when the Lord, besides whom there is no Savior, repeatedly and earnestly calls, He often calls in vain.

People's hearts are dull, their ears deaf, and they refuse to acknowledge Him.

We can never sufficiently lament that sin has made many madmen in the world. Life and death, blessing and curse are set before them, but men choose death before life. The most astonishing and intolerable curses are embraced, while permanent blessings of the highest nature are rejected.[1] Thus, the Lord reasons not only in reference to sin, but in reference to punishment. In His appeal to the "house of Israel," He not only asks why they dare to transgress His law but also asks why they are so ready to die.

At the beginning of Ezekiel 33, the Lord appoints Ezekiel as a watchman over the house of Israel. He is commanded to lift up his voice when he sees the revenging sword drawn and ready to cut off the ungodly. Unless the watchman calls to the wicked to turn and live, he is an accessory to their death. If he does not warn, their blood will be required at his hand. Commissioned by God, the watchman is commanded to stop the mouths of evildoers who cavil against their Maker and, in effect, foolishly charge God.

---

1. In the original, Vincent includes the following Latin statement: "Pro superi! Quantam mortalia pectora caecae, Noctis habent!" Roughly translated this reads: "Oh heavens! How great is the night possessed by the mortal minds of the blind!" He is quoting from the *Metamorphoses* of Publius Ovidius Naso.

It is apparent that there was disagreement about who should be blamed for the destruction of sinners. The house of Israel very emphatically and boldly placed the blame on God, saying that the way of the Lord is not equal. But the God of mercy and truth vindicates Himself from their unjust charge and declares that if sinners were not perversely bent on their own ruin, they could escape any impending destruction. God swears upon His own life that the death of the wicked does not please Him. So, in this text, His voice is loud and repeated: "Turn ye, turn ye from your evil ways; for why will ye die, O house of Israel?" In this passage the "saddle is set upon the right horse";[2] men's own wills are the cause of their woe.

The words in this passage express a very emotional and serious call. Several particulars may be observed:

- The persons called are the house of Israel.

- They are called to turn.

- The call is urgent, evident from the repeated phrase: "Turn ye, turn ye."

- The call requires a turning from their evil ways.

- God's call to turn is persuasive. An abundance of holy rhetoric is included in the argument, "Why will ye die?"

---

2. An idiom meaning "to set the blame on the true offender."

Without turning, death is certain. Although Satan may claim—as he did once to our first parents—"Ye shall not surely die" (Gen. 3:4), this will be found true: those "shall be turned into hell" who will not turn to God (Ps. 9:17). Every evil way will end in death. While there are several paths that comprise the broad way, they all conclude and meet in death, namely, the second death. In His grace, the Lord pities sinners and pleads with them, "Why will you die?" He asks, as it were, "Will you die because I am so quick to revenge? You know that I am slow to anger, and you know it by experience—if it were not so, I would have poured out My wrath on you long ago. Or will you die because I am relentless, not to be entreated when once provoked? I have often proclaimed Myself ready to forgive and full of mercy unto everyone who calls upon Me. Will you die because no one has ever told you the way to recover life, or because you do not know how to fly from the punishment you deserve? How often have I sent My prophets that you might believe, repent, and obey? But still you seek death; you are resolved to rush on in sin. If you perish, you may thank yourselves. If you are destroyed, it is because you chose destruction."

Ezekiel 33:11 provides us with three doctrines that we will examine in the subsequent chapters. We will outline these doctrines and their applications as follows:

- The way of evil is the way of death (chapter 2).

- Men die as a result of their own will (chapter 3).

- The Lord repeatedly calls sinners to turn from their evil ways and live (chapter 4).

- Applications of these doctrines (chapter 5).

The Way of Evil Is the Way of Death

The first doctrine we can draw from Ezekiel 33:11 is that every evil way leads to death. In other words, the pathway of moral evil is destructive to those who walk in it. Even though evil paths may seem right, they are to be considered dangerous. Scripture affirms, "There is a way which seemeth right unto a man, but the end thereof are the ways of death" (Prov. 14:12).

The pathway of evil often accelerates and hastens temporal death. That was the sentence God pronounced upon man's fall: "Dust thou art, and unto dust shalt thou return" (Gen. 3:19). Often the execution of this sentence is hurried because of sin. In fact, Scripture speaks of some who will "not live out half their days" because of their wickedness (Ps. 55:23). Those who fell and decayed in the wilderness might have lived to possess the land of promise were it not for their murmuring. At times they committed idolatry and fornication, and in the end God swore an oath that they should not enter Canaan. How the intemperate and unclean waste their strength and punish themselves with so many diseases! And though miserably unprepared for judgment, they hasten their departure out of this world to the tribunal of Him who judges righteously.

God, who is our life, is not found in the way of evil. Though physically alive while we walk upon this earth, we are spiritually dead. Scripture says the Ephesians were dead in trespasses and sins while they walked according to the course of this world and had their conversation in the lusts of their flesh (Eph. 2:1–3). If the soul's life consists in being united to God, in being animated and acted upon by His Spirit, then iniquity that separates us from God must be counted as a deadly thing (Isa. 59:2).

The evil ways indicated in this verse are the beaten path to hell's damnation, to everlasting death. No one ever came to hell except through these ways, and everyone who continues to walk in them without turning will end there. The enemy upon the pale horse is certainly dreadful, but when hell—as the second horse—follows immediately after, who can stand strong? No heart can endure hell. One of the Fathers called this second death the "deathless death,"[1] or "the death that is immortal," because the sinner is never delivered from his pain; he is always tortured, but never released. The fire still burns,

---

1. Greek: *thanatos athanatos.*

but never consumes its victim; the worm still gnaws, but is never satisfied.

O blinded soul, why are you rushing wildly onward? Is it gain, delight, and happiness that you seek? While you may imagine that you are pursuing this, if you persist to dash along the broad way, it is not gain, but loss; not pleasure, but pain; not happiness, but extreme misery that will be your reward. Stop your course and leave this lower path (Prov. 15:24)! Depart from the way to hell and instead wisely seek the way to life that is above.

The Righteousness of God Displayed in the Punishment of Death

As we have already seen, the way of evil is the way of death. But some may question whether this is just. God's righteousness in punishing evildoers with death is evident in numerous ways. First, evil ways are expressly forbidden by Him, the supreme lawgiver, the One who has power to save and to destroy. Should man, weak and wretched as he is, affront and despise God's majesty and authority that is so infinitely above him, he justly deserves infinite punishment. Furthermore, the Lord presents and offers Himself to sinners if they will forsake their evil ways and thoughts; if a sinner rejects that offer, preferring the empty world and vile lusts before the blessed God, reason itself declares it right that the impenitent sinner be eternally separated from Him.

This "pain of loss,"[2] or loss of God, is properly the death spoken of here; it is the very hell of hell.

Secondly, sinners are threatened with death. If they continue on the path that brings them under the lash of punishment, it is just and right that they should experience the pain that results from their presumption. Sinners are warned to flee from the wrath to come, and if they do not heed this warning, that promised wrath will justly overtake them. They cannot plead that they did not know their Master's will or that they were ignorant of the penalty for their rebellion. Those who enjoy the gospel's light but do not bow under it have often been informed it is God's will that they sorrow and repent of their sin. Even more, they know it is God's will that they believe in His Son, and they know that He desires their sanctification (1 Thessalonians 4). They have often been warned of the punishment to be endured by those who continue in willful disobedience. As they have accused the Lord of being a liar with their continued unbelief, it is fitting and just that He vindicate His truth; it is just that He cause them to feel those plagues and torments, for they ignored His many warnings.

Thirdly, sinners are not only threatened with death if they continue in their evil ways, they are also shown the way of life and peace, a much preferred path to walk. God freely offers strengthening grace to sinners. But if the

---

2. Latin: *poena damni.*

sinner disregards the glory and immortality promised at the end of the way and rejects that help and grace offered along the way, but instead prefers the path of destruction and misery (Rom. 3:16), he wrongs his own soul. God is thus righteous in destroying the defiant sinner.

Warning against the Way of Death

The one use I will make of this doctrine is to caution you against these evil ways that are the ways of death. You who have, through grace, left them, take heed of declining toward them. Many saints have paid significant costs when they have stepped aside. Their falls have defiled them and broken their bones. Those of you who still resolve to walk in these ways, open your eyes and see where you are going! Upon reading these lines, stop without delay for fear that sudden death, destruction, and damnation come upon you, and there is no possibility of escape (1 Thess. 5:3).

Do not let the so-called profit of evil ways blind you. Riches are deceitful; they appear to be what they are not, and while we are eagerly pursuing them we are tricked and cheated of far truer riches. Running after earthly treasure, we miss heavenly treasure that will never fail (Luke 12:33). Do not be deluded by mammon. While evil ways may promise satisfaction, ease, and contentment, the result can only be trouble and vexation. The Lord likens riches to thorns, partly because they tend to choke the good seed of the Word, and partly because they pierce those who idolize them. If you were to take God's just balances and weigh the gain of your evil ways, and compare this with the loss that you do and will sustain, it would become apparent that Satan's heart and the sinful heart's plea of profit is very unreasonable. Although the sinner may gain the earth, he loses God's grace; he may gain gold, but loses God. If you persist in your evil way you may gain a little of the world—something to be kept for a little while—but you lose your soul and eternal glory.

Do not let the pleasures of these evil ways ensnare you. The pleasures of sin usually delight only the more brutish part of man. A rational human being acts below himself when he nurses pleasures that are shared by the beasts. Solomon had an abundance of them. Whatever his eyes desired, he gave them; he did not withhold his heart from any joy. But later he found these pleasures to be so meaningless, so base and unsuitable, that, in the midst of them, he cried out, "All [is] vanity and vexation of spirit" (Eccl. 2:10–11). Pleasures may seem like delightful dreams, but they are short-lived. Affliction and death, or hell itself, soon awaken us. Those who love pleasure more than God do not really know what they choose and what they refuse. Promised pleasure is the bait that covers sin, causing us to swallow it with eagerness. It is the fatal potion that stupefies you and makes you lie senseless while in extreme danger. Promised pleasures are the fine—but very strong—cord that Satan uses to draw men down to the chambers of death. Indeed, they are the fuel that heats the burning lake. Revelation 18:7 states, "How much she hath glorified herself, and lived deliciously, so much torment and sorrow give her." It is certain that one day sensual persons will experience eternal pain for all their fleeting pleasures!

Do not let the multitude of evildoers sway or harden you. Lot walked alone in the way of righteousness even though Sodom was generally defiled by ungodly behavior. He would not follow a multitude to do evil. Christ said, "Strait is the gate, and narrow is the way, which leadeth unto life, and few there be that find it" (Matt. 7:14), but He never intended that His disciples should tread along the beaten path of the world. Sinner, do not deceive yourself. If you sinfully do what others do, your reward will be as theirs; together you will be cast into hell for your wickedness.

In hell it will be no comfort to have companions in your misery, but rather among the damned there will be a torturing grief and indignation at the sight of each other as each recalls what incarnate devils the others were to his soul and how they helped forward his condemnation. This may have been the reason why the rich man of Luke 16 was so unwilling that his brothers should come to his place of torment; if he was damned for sins that he assented to and committed with them in his lifetime, their company with him in hell would have only added to his anguish. We commonly say in this life,

"The more, the merrier," but in hell it will be, "The more, the sadder." When God has all of His enemies in one place and none of His people are mingled with them, then His fierce wrath will be stirred up and He will pour out His fury upon them.

CHAPTER 3

Death as a Result of One's Choice

The second doctrine that we can draw from Ezekiel 33:11 is this: the great reason why men die (and die forever), is because they will it. They choose to be servants of sin, even though death is the only wage they will have for their weary and toilsome service. As Jeremiah 13:27 makes clears, sinners do not desire cleansing: "Woe unto thee, O Jerusalem! wilt thou not be made clean? when shall it once be?" Sinners do not want to be gathered under the wing of Christ, despite this being the only place of refuge from both the rage of Satan and the wrath of God. Matthew 23:37 states, "O Jerusalem, Jerusalem, thou that killest the prophets, and stonest them which are sent unto thee, how often would I have gathered thy children together, even as a hen gathereth her chickens under her wings, and ye would not!" The wills of many who have often rejected the admonitions and calls of Moses and the Prophets are so desperately bent to sin that, even if they should see the torments of hell, they would not be persuaded to forsake it. This is certainly evident from Luke 16:30–31: "Nay, father Abraham: but if one went unto them from the dead, they will repent. And he said unto him, If they hear not Moses and the prophets, neither will they be persuaded, though one rose from the dead."

In our consideration of this doctrine in this chapter, I will focus on three thoughts: first, the truth of man's willingness to die must be demonstrated; second, I argue that man's inability to do good, so often spoken of in Scripture, does not contradict or undermine this doctrine; and third, I will show the value or use of this doctrine.

The Truth of This Doctrine Established

There are two principal arguments that demonstrate that men's own wills are the great cause of their death and perdition. The first argument is drawn from the natural corruption and depravation of the will of man. It must be understood that this corruption finds its root in the will's conscious turning from God—who is the fountain of life and peace—and instead inclining to what is evil. This is, of course, not how the sinner views his condition; the sinner calls evil good and imagines that which is bitter and poisonous to be sweet. Pelagians have compared the human will to a young woman who professes her pure virginity despite an instance of unfaithfulness, but it is certain, from both Scripture and experience, that original sin affects the will. The one who does not understand his heart to be desperately wicked is deceived (Jer. 17:9), and he is unacquainted with his own heart. Consider the unbelief, pride, alienation from the life of God, and enmity against His holy, just, and good command there is in a natural man's will (Romans 7). The will, so utterly corrupted and possessing the influence it does, does everything in its power to hinder conversion to God and holiness. Because the will dislikes God and holiness so much, it has a great hand in the perdition of the children of men.

The second argument that demonstrates this doctrine's truth is drawn from the justness of God's reproof and anger. Certainly God would not so sharply rebuke sinners, His anger would not smoke so severely against their stubbornness and willful persistence in evil ways, if they had a sincere will and lacked only the power to do good. When the Lord inflicted judgment on Israel in the Old Testament, He lamented their obstinacy and their refusal to listen to Him and turn back. In essence, their refusal to turn justified the severe ways in which He dealt with them. We read in 2 Kings 17:13–14, 18 that the Lord testified against Israel by His prophets and seers saying, "Turn ye from your evil ways, and keep my commandments…. Notwithstanding they would not hear, but hardened their necks, like to the neck of their fathers, that did not believe in the LORD their God." Understandably and very justly, their willful disobedience resulted in God's anger and their destruction.

Due to their unwillingness, the Lord was very angry with the children of Israel and removed them from His sight.

Our Inability to Do Good Is Not an Excuse

Secondly, our inability to do good does not undermine the doctrine that one's sin and misery is a direct result of one's will. The Holy Spirit, in order to humble the children of men and beat down their opinion of their own power and righteousness, makes them confess, "Surely… in the LORD have I righteousness and strength" (Isa. 45:24); the Spirit instructs us that man, in his sinful and degenerate state, is unable to do anything that is spiritually good. Therefore, as Paul teaches, we are said to be without strength (Rom. 5:6); elsewhere he writes, "Not that we are sufficient of ourselves to think any thing as of ourselves; but our sufficiency is of God" (2 Cor. 3:5). Scripture further tells us we are faint and have no might (Isa. 40:29), and our Lord tells us plainly in John 15:5, "Without me ye can do nothing." Nevertheless, although we lack power to do good, our wills are to blame for the evil we do.

We should not imagine that Scripture teaches about sinners' inability to do good in order to provide them with an excuse for committing evil. Rather, this should drive us to Christ, who can strengthen us to do all things (Phil. 4:13). It is true that sinful man is unable to do good, but despite this, he is unwilling to do what God requires of him, even if it is for his own benefit.

The reason why he continues in sin and is destroyed by it is not only because he cannot convert himself, but also—and more principally—because he is unwilling to be converted. This truth is made further apparent in the following three particulars.

First, sinful man imagines he is able to turn himself from his evil ways. Thus, he puts off his repentance as if he could turn to God at a moment's notice. But he does not do what he thinks he can, so his own will must be the impediment; it is his will that he must blame if he perishes.

Second, sinful man will not do what he is truly able to perform. In other words, sinful man will not trade for the one talent he has. There are many sins—sins that expose him to wrath and vengeance—that he might abstain from if he chose, but he voluntarily enslaves himself to them and is, in fact, pleased with this servitude. The adulterer willfully seeks out illegitimate sexual pleasure, and the unrighteous business owner willfully accumulates dishonest gain. It follows that unrepentant sinners willfully destroy themselves.

It should be noted that while a natural man can do good with respect to the *matter* of a thing, he fails in the *manner* of doing it. He can pray, hear, and read, but he willfully omits these duties, and so willfully subjects himself to the curse threatened upon omitting them. He will not do what he truly can, and even if his abilities were increased, he would not use them. If a wealthy person refuses to give a penny to the poor, we may conclude that he would be also unwilling to give a dollar (or any other larger amount). Similarly, a natural man who will not do whatever he can to be saved (however little this may be), would not do any more in order to attain his salvation were his powers enlarged.

Third, a sinful and unrepentant man is sorry that he is able to do what he can. Indeed, the sinner wishes that he were totally impotent; then he would have an excuse. This demonstrates the wickedness of the sinner's will. Furthermore, the sinner will not use the means by which God conveys grace and strength. The unrepentant sinner will not wait and call on God; he will not ask God to accomplish the promises made in His gracious covenant. Instead, he willfully resists the Spirit when He comes to work on him and would rather be left alone in sin. This is precisely the desire of the ungodly expressed in Job 21:14: "They say unto God, Depart from us; for we desire not the knowledge of thy ways." The wicked man, though he may complain that he lacks power, is ruined by his lack of will to be turned and live.

What is to be made of all those high thoughts and reasonings against God, thoughts that make Him out to be a hard and unjust master? Surely the sinner will be ashamed of them at the great day. Then his conscience will convict him, and sadness will reproach him as he considers that he was often warned and called to turn, but he would not turn and live.

The Use or Value of This Doctrine

A Word of Reason

If it is true that men die forever because they will it, then who are you to charge God with destruction? Surely in this you charge God foolishly. As He does not delight in your sin, so also He does not delight in your death. The criminal must not be angry with a judge for pronouncing a sentence of condemnation, but he should rather blame himself for doing that which deserves to be punished. How often has the Lord called, but you refused? How often has He stretched out His hand to you, and yet you remain disobedient and contrary? How speechless you will be when He comes to judge the world in righteousness!

If it is true that men die forever because they will it, then the death of the wicked is most just and righteous. It is fitting that chains of darkness should eternally bind willing slaves of sin—those who would not be freed by the Lord. An offender who refuses a pardon doubly deserves judgment, both because of his offense and because he scoffs at mercy. Just as the patient who pushes away the physician deserves to die from his disease, so too the sinner who will not turn to God, who rejects the Lord Jesus who is able to pardon and heal, is not in the least wronged when he perishes and is condemned.

If it is true that men die forever because they will it, how torturous will it be in hell to know that it was their own willfulness that brought them there. These reflections will be like many poisoned daggers that pierce the soul of a damned reprobate. What provoked me to listen to the devil? Why did I side with Satan only to bring about my own destruction? How foolish I was to make the whips with which I am eternally to be lashed, to kindle the flames in which I must dwell and burn forever!

A Word of Caution

Two notes of caution are especially worth your consideration: (1) be careful not to sin willfully, which is the pathway leading to death; and (2) be careful not to content yourselves with a seeming willingness to escape destruction. First, let me caution you against willful sinning. The more that the will is involved in transgression, the greater the provocation. Thus, David is very earnest to be kept from presumptuous sins because presumptuous sins are so great (Ps. 19:13). In a time of much knowledge, do not be willfully ignorant. With all of the helps and encouragements to duty we enjoy, do not be lazy (a fault of the will), but imitate those who through faith and patience inherited the promises (Heb. 6:12). Do not let sin be loved, pleaded for, or lived in. Do not let the pleasing taste of forbidden fruit entice you to disobey; do not let its fine-colored skin or texture cause you to embrace a serpent, one who will sting you to death.

Secondly, let me caution you against only a seeming willingness to turn from sin and escape destruction. An idle, industrious will is only a seeming will. A lazy wish to be saved (where there is no serious use of the means of salvation), only signifies that you are grossly ignorant and stupid—ignorant of the worth of salvation and stupidly insensible of your own danger.

Likewise, a will for the future is only a seeming will. Most who walk in evil ways have a future desire to leave them, but this only shows their present unwillingness. And, if you are opposed to turning now, you will likely be even more averse to turning when God is further away from you, when Satan has a stronger foothold in you, when conscience is grown more stupid, and when habits of sin have doubled your natural inclination to it. Just think how many millions have died and been taken away in their iniquities who were as fully resolved upon future repentance as you are or anyone else alive today. Be careful to not fall on this rock that has split so many, people who are then cast away forever. God's will is for the present. He says, "To day if ye will hear [My] voice, harden not your hearts" (Heb. 3:7–8). But if you are unwilling now, when God is willing to give you life, after this life He will be unwilling when you desire it. When death and destruction come upon you as a whirlwind, He warns that though you will call upon Him for life and salvation, it will be far from you. As Proverbs 1:28–29 states, "They shall seek me early, but they shall not find me: for that they hated knowledge, and did not choose the fear of the LORD."

Furthermore, a will founded upon a mistake is also only a seeming will. Those whom our Lord compared to the stony ground heard the word with joy and were willing to embrace it, but they did not dream of the cross and persecution that accompany it. That made them fall away. Many seem to be willing converts, but they do not sit down and count the cost of conversion. Many very quickly become unwilling once they are informed that they must deny themselves, that they must let go of all their current affections and possessions that compete for supremacy with the Lord Jesus. Many, when informed that they must put to death every lust, despite its offer of delight or gain; when informed to watch, pray, and walk with the greatest care, fervency, and circumspection; and when told that they must take the kingdom of heaven with a holy violence or else fall short and lose their crown, then they fall away crying out, "These are hard sayings, who can hear them?"

A Word of Exhortation

Since men die because they will it, let me persuade you of the need for the renewal of your will. Man has no worse enemy than his own will (that is, until a change is worked in it). In order that this change may be effected, observe these four directions:

(1) Consider and judge your own natural perverseness. Until you are aware of this, you cannot be properly humbled. That you have

sinned so much and so long should very much affect and afflict you before God, but that you have a will to sin ten thousand times more (but for the restraints of grace), even to sin unto eternity, should cause sorrow and confusion.

(2) Study the deceitfulness of the tempter and the world. Then your heart will not be so enticed with their baits and consequently drawn away from God. The world is vain and vexing, and Satan is a liar and a murderer. You have little reason to yield to either.

(3) Set before your eyes both the blessedness of eternal life and the misery of everlasting death; choose to walk in the way leading to life.

Be constant in prayer that the Lord, according to His promise, would give you a new heart and work in you to will of His own good pleasure (Ezek. 36:26; Phil. 2:13). And if He causes your heart to desire grace and glory, He will satisfy them as He raised them in you. If He works in you to will and to do, despite all opposition, you will work out your own salvation, and He will administer an abundant entrance into His everlasting kingdom (2 Peter 1:11).

CHAPTER 4

The Lord's Repeated Call to
Turn from Death to Life

The third doctrine that we can draw from Ezekiel 33:11 is that the Lord repeatedly calls sinners to turn from their evil ways and live. "Turn ye, turn ye," says God in the text. The business of conversion is not something man first thought of. He would never think of it or be persuaded to it if the Lord did not call after him and make that call effectual. In Scripture we read of penitent persons crying and begging to be turned, but these cries merely echo God's voice and initial call. In handling this doctrine, I will first show how God calls sinners to turn to Him; second, why He does it; and third, explain the nature of this conversion or turning. The final chapter will conclude with further applications of this doctrine.

How God Calls Sinners to Turn

In the first place I am to show how God calls upon sinners to turn to Him. In this section I will outline five ways in which God calls sinners to turn to Him.

God Calls from Mount Ebal (The Call of the Law)

First, God calls sinners to turn from Mount Ebal, the mountain from which God's curses were denounced. In His Word God warns of the cursedness and misery of the unconverted state. He sends the law as a schoolmaster to teach unrepentant sinners a sad lesson, warning them that because of their frequent transgressions they are teetering upon the brink of eternal misery. His goal is that they may be awakened and stopped in their destructive path, and that they would not flatter themselves with hopes of peace despite walking after the imaginations of their own heart.

This voice of the Lord by the law is loud and terrible, uttered on purpose to rouse and startle those who are fatally asleep. When the law was delivered, "the mount...burned with fire," and there was "blackness, and darkness, and tempest, and the sound of a trumpet, and the voice of words; which voice they that heard intreated that the word should not be spoken to them any more.... And so terrible was the sight, that Moses said, I exceedingly fear and quake" (Heb. 12:18–19, 21). Moreover, if the manner of the law's delivery is considered dreadful, the law's execution upon those who violate it will be much more dreadful. The fire and darkness at Mount Sinai were nothing compared to the fire of hell and its utter blackness. Upon the impenitently wicked the Lord has threatened to "rain snares, fire and brimstone, and an horrible tempest: this shall be the portion of their cup" (Ps. 11:6). Certainly this lecture of the law is necessary so that we attain a true knowledge and understanding of sin. It is only when we have been at the foot of Mount Ebal and Sinai and have heard that sin results in the denial of many blessings, and instead brings numerous curses—temporal, spiritual, and everlasting—that we can know the cure to our unreasonable devotion to sin; only then do we fear and tremble because we have given in to sin so much.

God Calls from Mount Gerizim
(The Call of the Gospel)

Second, God calls sinners from Mount Gerizim, the mountain from which many blessings have sounded. God not only warns sinners of impending wrath that threatens while they continue in iniquity, but He also invites them to consider His mercy, a mercy that will be brought near to them on condition that they forsake their wickedness. God promises mercy and abundant pardon to the righteous man when he forsakes his sinful ways and thoughts (Isa. 55:7). This call of the gospel from Mount Gerizim is like the still voice after the strong wind, the fire, and the earthquake. The words of Zechariah 1:3 are full of encouragement: "'Turn ye unto me, saith the LORD of hosts, and I will turn unto you." Hosea 14:1 also states, "O Israel, return unto the LORD thy God; for thou hast fallen by thy iniquity." Elsewhere the Lord says, "O Israel, thou hast destroyed thyself; but in me is thine help" (Hos. 13:9). Although you deserve nothing but the Lord's anger and hatred, He declares, "I will heal their backsliding, I will love them freely" (Hos. 14:4).

Satan, by tempting us to sin, has taken away our blessing from us; nevertheless, we do not need to despair, as the Lord has more than one blessing. The blessing that the first Adam forfeited, the second Adam was sent to restore. Acts 3:26 records, "God, having raised up his Son Jesus, sent him to bless you, in turning away every one of you from his iniquities." It is as if the Lord takes sinners up to the top of Mount Gerizim and shows them His kingdom and all its glory. He tells them of His abundant blessings, of the inestimable benefits purchased by His Son—justification, adoption, sanctification, and glory—and assures them that all of this will be theirs if they will turn to Him. Truly, this a very different offer than Satan makes, or possibly can make.

God Calls with Passionate Pleas

Third, God calls sinners to turn with the most fervent pleas and pressing arguments. His design in these pleas and arguments is to make sinners sensible of their unreasonableness in pursuing deceitful vanities and defiled lusts, and to show how foolish it is to refuse to convert unto Him who can both sanctify them from their defilements and satisfy them with His all-sufficiency. Thus, He reasons, for example, with Judah in Isaiah

55:2, asking them, "Wherefore do ye spend money for that which is not bread? and your labour for that which satisfieth not?" It is as if He were saying, "Since coming to Me, you obtain the life of your souls and the sure mercies of an everlasting covenant; do not settle for less."

The Lord pleads with the ungodly by the ministry of the word in this manner: "What! Although you are told of sin's deceitful, defiling, and damnable nature, will you still embrace and hold tightly to it and thus bring dishonor to Me and destruction upon yourself? Although you are warned of the heat and heaviness of My anger, will you not run from it? Although you are often informed of the pain and suffering in hell, will you run there and so burn forever? Although told of a kingdom that cannot be moved, will you not be moved with desire for it? Will you not be persuaded to strive to enter this kingdom? Are grace and glory of no value to you? Should not a Savior be prized by them who are enslaved and lost in sin and are in danger of being lost for eternity? Consider these things, and show yourselves to be men, O transgressors!" In this manner the Lord pleads with sinners, desiring that He may prevail upon them for their own good.

God Calls through Examples

Fourth, God calls sinners to turn through the example of others, and especially through the rod that falls heavily upon others. The ungodly are prone to observe bad examples in order to imitate them, but they must note when God inflicts exemplary punishments on others, and so be afraid to follow them in wickedness any longer. When we see others plagued for the sins of which we are guilty, the Lord invites us—using the pain felt by others—to see the heinousness of our own iniquity. And we may justly expect that our sins will have a similar end if we continue in that path. Examples are purposely set before us so that we do not lust after evil things (1 Cor. 10:6), and so that we turn away from the paths that have led others to ruin.

But it is especially when the rod falls upon our own backs that God calls us to turn to Him in a more perceivable and recognizable way. The design of the rod is to cause sin to be bitter for both the flesh and the conscience; as sin is the cause of every stripe, we no longer think of it as delightful. The rod, like the word, has a voice, and it is wise to listen to it. When the sinner is afflicted, the Lord speaks as, for example, in Jeremiah 2:17: "Hast thou not procured this unto thyself?" To turn from your iniquity is for your own good; let the pain of the rod (which is nothing compared to the pains of hell) convince you not to admire sin for its feigned pleasure. At present you are only chastised with whips, but if you remain persistent in your sin, surely you will be lashed with scorpions.

God Calls by His Spirit

Finally—and we will treat this fifth point more exten-sively—God calls sinners to turn to Him by the internal voice and motions of His Spirit. The Spirit often warns of the false way of sin, "This is not the way; therefore, turn from it." But concerning the way of holiness that leads to God, the Spirit says, "This is the way, walk ye in it" (Isa. 30:21). All of the other calls already discussed will be of little use unless the Spirit accompanies them. Without His conviction, the pronouncement of curses will not awaken; without His illumination, the offered blessings will be undervalued; without His persuasion, the most stirring reasons will not have an effect, and the loudest words will be like a whisper; and without His teaching and instruction, the rod will be mute and insignificant. The evildoer will not learn anything, either by personal affliction or by national judgments, without the Spirit. It is dangerous, therefore, to disregard or resist the Holy Spirit since the efficacy of God's call depends on Him.

The Twofold Call of the Holy Spirit: Common and Special

There is a call that is more common, and so many are called who never are truly converted. It was the common work of the Spirit that made Felix tremble, brought Agrippa within a step of Christianity, and caused Herod to do many things. Many unregenerate people feel the waters stirred; the Holy Spirit, moving them to conversion, readily offers His aid and assistance, and, perhaps, for a short time they are led by Him. But then they refuse to let go of some lust or vanity that He calls them to abandon. They will not turn their spiritual sloth into serious and diligent concern about their immortal souls, and so, by disregarding Him and slighting His help, they cause the Spirit to leave in grief, the One who came in love to work on them.

But there is also a call of the Spirit that is special and efficacious; in this case He does not *almost* move sinners to turn to God, but He *altogether* persuades them to believe. In the remainder of this section we will examine the method by which the Spirit works on those who are indeed made converts.

It is certainly the case that those whom the Spirit calls effectually, He convinces of sin (John 16:8). Not only does He set the law before them, but He Himself is the law's interpreter. By His commentary, they see that the law forbids not only the outward display of sin from their lips or in their lives, but also the inward expressions of sin in their heart (i.e., lust or the desire to sin). The offense abounds even more when the law is explained this way. The Spirit sets their iniquities before them, opening their eyes to see their sin. The book of conscience is opened, and the sinner sees how many transgressions are registered there. If, upon dipping into this book, so many abominations appear, imagine what an innumerable multitude are recorded in the book of God's remembrance! Though sinners may soon forget, God remembers all their wickedness (Hos. 7:2). The awakened soul lays to heart David's words of Psalm 40:12: "For innumerable evils have compassed me about: mine iniquities have taken hold upon me." Wherever the sinner goes, his sins doggedly haunt him; when he lies down, they lie down, and when he rises, they rise with him.

If the sinner has lived a notorious life, sin will appear hideous and horrid when all pleas and excuses are silenced, when the painted visor is pulled off and sin is viewed in all of its ugliness. Drunkenness, uncleanness, swearing, profanity, and worldly greediness will no longer be taken lightly. Sins such as these seemed to pose no danger before, but instead were thought to produce much delight and pleasure. But after the Spirit's conviction, their deceitful and damnable nature will be as evident as the noonday sun.

And even if the sinner has been free from the more obvious pollutions of the world, yet enough will be shown him so that he concludes he is a wretch and in a lost estate. Is his disdain and even mocking of the jealous God counted as nothing? Is his misuse of time and disregard for eternity nothing? Is his vain delight in creatures and the things of this world—a love that is greater than his care for God, Christ, and glory—a small matter? These are indeed heinous sins, sins that even respectable people are guilty of.

In someone who is effectually called, this conviction of the Spirit is strong and lasting. It does not wear off before the sinner is brought home. Actual transgressions are aggravating and lie heavy on them, and original sin is seen to be the fountain from which this actual sin flows. Sinners recognize that this fountain is able to feed ten thousand times more streams than it has; thus, David is not only convinced of the murder and adultery he committed, but he traces these sins to its source, the original corruption of his nature (Ps. 51:5). This realization greatly increased his humiliation.

Finally, this conviction is not only of some acts of sin, but of the corruption of the sinner's estate. The Spirit shows the sinner that he is a child of disobedience, a child of wrath. Without complaining or objecting the sinner yields to and acknowledges as true the Spirit's judgment of himself; this is evidence of the Spirit's convicting work.

The Spirit also works fear in those He effectually calls. The "spirit of bondage to fear" precedes the "Spirit of adoption" (Rom. 8:15). While these fears and terrors are present in everyone according to varying degrees, enough is present in each person whom the Lord chooses to love so as to make them restless in their natural estate. Carnal security is one of the first things wounded by the Spirit. He calls the soul to wake up, warning the sinner that to sleep in sin is much more hazardous, even, than sleeping on the top of a ship's mast.

The sinner should be afraid. He has set wrath against himself, wrath that is armed with irresistible and almighty power. "Who can stand before his indignation? and who can abide in the fierceness of his anger?" (Nah. 1:6). The curses of the law have a dreadful sound in the sinner's ears; the threat of damnation is imminent. The nearness of such great evil raises his fear exceedingly. In his mind he foresees "the Lord Jesus... revealed from heaven with his mighty angels, in flaming fire taking vengeance on them that know not God, and that obey not the gospel of our Lord Jesus Christ: who shall be punished with everlasting destruction" (2 Thess. 1:7–9). He thinks to himself: "How terrible it will be to, with those on the final day, call on the rocks and mountains to fall upon us so that we may hide from the face of Him who sits on the throne, and from the wrath of the Lamb!" These thoughts stop him in his wicked course. He does not dare rush into sin, unlike the horse who rushes into battle.

Furthermore, the Spirit stimulates grief and sorrow due to sin in those whom He effectually calls. Those called by the Spirit see what they have done against God and themselves, and this troubles their hearts. This is what Scripture refers to when it directs the weary and "heavy laden" to find rest for their souls in Christ (Matt. 11:28–29). Jeremiah 3:21 records, "A voice was heard upon the high places, weeping and supplications of the children of Israel: for they have perverted their way, and they have forgotten the LORD their God." This verse precedes verse 22, which includes God's invitation to return to Him. The Spirit causes the sinner to see the sadness of his state, the evil of sin, how miserably he has been deceived by his desires and by Satan, and consequently his own foolishness in yielding to them. He now accuses and condemns himself. His heart is grieved and his conscience pricked because he has been so ignorant and foolish; he has acted like a beast before God (Ps. 73:21–22). He wishes a thousand times that he had refused temptations and that he had never committed sin.

The sinner laments in his heart, "Oh, what a wretch I am! What have I done all my days? Was I made to destroy myself? Did I not have anything better to do than to add sin to sin, and so pile up wrath to be displayed on the final day of judgment? How much time have I misspent, and what pains have I taken to make myself miserable! Foolish, self-destroying wretch! Do you not see how much you have provoked the Lord to anger? If only my head was water and my eyes fountains of tears, that I might weep day and night! The damned will weep and wail forever. Should I, who deserve to be damned, not mourn and weep? I would do well to be troubled and greatly humbled and mourn all day long." So the sinner grieves; and carnal company, sensual pleasures, and worldly diversions cannot drive this sorrow away. Only the Spirit, who broke his heart, is able to bind up and heal its wounds.

When the Spirit effectually calls, He causes people to despair of themselves. They perceive that they themselves have no power to climb out of the sinful and miserable depths into which they have plunged. And as they are unable to help themselves, they also see that they are utterly unworthy of help. God may justly allow them to lie where they are fallen; if this is His sovereign choice, they will fall lower and lower until they are past recovery. The sinner called by the Spirit may return to performing his duties, hoping to appease God for what he has done wrong, but the Spirit causes him to see that his best actions have so much sin mingled with them that, were it not for Christ's righteousness and intercession, they would be an abomination. Thus, he is beaten off from standing on his own foundation. As Paul says, he no longer has confidence in the flesh (Phil. 3:3); he can do nothing of himself and can claim nothing as his reward, but must instead attribute everything to free grace.

The called sinner cries out of the depths unto the Lord (Ps. 130:1). He perceives that he is sinking and cries, "Lord, save me or I perish. I am at the brink of the bottomless pit, and I will fall unless the hand of mercy catches hold of me." He begs with Ephraim, "Turn thou me, and I shall be turned" (Jer. 31:18). As the evil of sin is presented to him, the Spirit also, in some way, reveals to him the goodness of God. And so he desires to be converted not only out of necessity (otherwise he would be extremely and eternally miserable), but also because he is made willing and recognizes that this is the way to true happiness. These desires to be turned are the first breaths of the new creature.

Thus I have shown the manner of the Spirit's operation in those whom He effectually calls to turn to God. I have also shown other ways the Lord calls sinners to turn; these often prove ineffectual, especially if it is to those who are called deaf, disobedient, and contrary.

Why God Calls Sinners to Turn

Second, I wish to lay down the reasons why God calls the children of men to turn from their evil ways and live. Here I provide six reasons why God calls sinners to turn.

First, God's call to sinners is a demonstration of His gracious nature; He does not delight in the death and destruction of His creatures. Death will be inflicted on them because of their obstinate continuance in evil, but showing mercy and giving life are things that please God. So God calls even the most obstinate to conversion.

Second, the Lord calls us to turn so that He may inform us of our duty. From His call we understand that it is our duty not to stray, but to go quickly to our Father's house. And by the urgent frequency of the calls, the Lord emphasizes our obligation to this duty. If we disregard it and slight its great encouragements, our refusal to turn will do us more harm than all our other sins. Upon our conversion, the Lord would abundantly pardon all our other sins, but as long as we continue unconverted, not one sin is forgiven. Without turning, the guilt of every sin lies upon us, and we assuredly lie under wrath.

In the third place, the Lord calls us to turn to show that our conversion to Him will not be in vain. Though our sin abounds, yet there is not simply a possibility, but a certainty of being graciously received and embraced upon our return. This is a matter of great encouragement to someone who lies under the fear of sin and wrath. God says to Judah in Jeremiah 3:5 and 3:1: "Behold, thou hast spoken and done evil things as thou couldest." "Thou hast played the harlot with many lovers; yet return again to me, saith the LORD." This call demonstrates that Judah's transgressions, though multiplied greatly, would not cause the doors of mercy to shut against them if they would but genuinely turn to Him.

Fourth, the Lord calls sinners to turn in order to indicate that it is from Himself that we must have power and strength to turn in truth. Scripture's precepts and exhortations to convert, repent, believe, and stand fast (and others like it) are not given so that we might conclude we have power in ourselves to do what we are commanded to do, but that we might turn these precepts into prayers. For instance, when we hear the command to believe, it should make us cry out with the sick child's father in Mark 9:24, "Lord, I believe; help thou my unbelief." When we hear the command to put off every transgression, it should make us beg with David, "Order my steps in thy word: and let not any iniquity have dominion over me" (Ps. 119:133). When we hear the command to turn, it should produce in us language similar to the penitent in Jeremiah 31:18, who said, "Turn thou me, and I shall be turned; for thou art the LORD my God."

Fifth, the Lord calls us to turn so that the obstinate, who will not turn and will not come to Christ for life, are left without excuse. God said of Israel, "All day long have I stretched forth my hands unto a disobedient and gainsaying people" (Rom. 10:21), but their disobedience left them defenseless. How pitiful it will be when the unconverted fall into God's revenging hands. They will have nothing to plead because God's hands stretched out to them, inviting them with the gospel, was in vain. These sinners, who sin against their own souls, who are stubborn, who will not be terrified by threats, and who will not find comfort in the greatest display of kindness and mercy, will be struck speechless when God summons them to His judgment bar; they will not have one word to say against their condemnation. They were called to grace and glory, but they would not listen; they were told of their danger, but they did not seek to prevent it; they were informed and warned of their sinful ways—even passionately entreated to not harm themselves by yielding to sin—yet they did not desire to be freed from sin and become the servants of righteousness. Surely then their mouths must be stopped, or, if they say anything when their sentence is passed, it must be to agree with God's justice and to acknowledge the equality of His ways and the inequality of their own.

Finally, the Lord calls us to turn so that those ordained to eternal life may be effectually prevailed upon to turn. Scripture states that the gospel was preached both to the Jews and the Gentiles, "and as many as were ordained to eternal life believed" (Acts 13:48). Certainly the general nature of the call is largely because the elect are scattered throughout the vast number of people on the earth. All those whom the Father has given to Christ are brought home by this call and welcomed by Him. As John 6:37 makes clear, "All that the Father giveth me shall come to me; and him that cometh to me I will in no wise cast out."

The Nature of the Sinner's Conversion

I also must explain the nature of the sinner's conversion or turning. The apostle Paul gives a notable and full expression of it in Acts 26:18 when he says conversion is turning from darkness to light and turning from the power of Satan to God. From this we gather that conversion involves four things: being turned from darkness, being turned to light, being turned from the power of Satan, and being turned to God.

Conversion: Turning from Darkness

First, conversion includes being turned from darkness. As darkness was upon the face of the deep until God said, "Let there be light," so darkness is spread over the soul of natural man until he is enlightened from above. Believers are delivered from the power of darkness only when they are translated into the Son's kingdom (Col. 1:13). This translation means that at some point they were in darkness, a darkness that is equally over all natural men. This darkness is said to have a power; it has a power to hold, blind, and ruin. There is therefore a great need to be delivered from it. Those who turn are freed from several kinds of darkness. First, converts are turned from the darkness of ignorance. They are no longer content to be ignorant of the way to salvation, but desire to learn what they must do to be saved. They are informed about the doctrine of Christ and are made to understand what believing and repenting mean. They know that sin is the worst of evils, that God is the ultimate good, and that He "so loved the world, that he gave his only begotten Son, that whosoever believeth in him should not perish, but have everlasting life" (John 3:16). They are taught that Christ is to be received by faith, that salvation cannot be found in any other, and that it is hopeless to expect anything from Him as Savior unless one consents to obey Him as Lord. These truths, and others like them, are no longer hidden from those who turn. Converts are made aware of the damage and danger of ignorance. It is therefore their desire to have it completely removed and instead "follow on to know the LORD" (Hos. 6:3).

Converts are also turned from the darkness of unbelief. The Spirit persuades their hearts that whatever God has revealed in His Word is certain truth. They dare not make the Lord a liar any longer by not believing what He has recorded. They believe, admire, and acknowledge "the mystery of God, and of the Father, and of Christ" (Col. 2:2). Before turning to God, their unbelief hid the gospel from them, and it was evident they were lost. They did not see the mystery of the Word; they were not enamored with the treasures of wisdom and grace revealed in it; they were not concerned with the abundant terrors God's Word threatens against the ungodly. But when they turn, the veil is taken away, and they assent to and are affected by the gospel. They believe that God is in Christ reconciling the world to Himself, not imputing their trespasses to them, and that, being justified by His blood, they will be saved from wrath through Him (Rom. 5:9). They believe that sin is deadly and the world a cheat, and that solid and eternal happiness is to be found in God. They leave and reject a shadow and turn to embrace that which is substantial.

Converts are turned from the darkness of prejudice. Prejudice causes something like a strange mist that hinders the light of truth from shining into the mind. The Jews' prejudice against Christ was one great thing that blinded them, a primary obstacle to their conversion. Satan endeavors to fill the ungodly with these prejudices and to keep them up because they uphold his kingdom. Sometimes sinners are prejudiced against holiness, as if it were a disgrace. However, since holiness is the glory of the divine nature, it is certainly not a disgrace but the greatest honor and perfection that reasonable beings are capable of. Some look on holiness as useless, and yet Scripture affirms that no one will see the Lord without it. Sometimes the carnal heart rises against holiness because it imagines that delight and pleasure cannot accompany it, and yet in turning to God our joy is not lost, but only changed. The kingdom of God is not only righteousness, but also peace and joy in the Holy Spirit (Rom. 14:17). The joy we had before was poor, low, ruthless, and defiling; it was mixed with many secret complaints of conscience and reservations of heart. But upon conversion, the joy is pure, angelical, satisfying, and a deposit of those "pleasures [which will be] for evermore" (Ps. 16:11).

The unconverted are not only prejudiced against the way of holiness, but also against those who publish or speak of this way. The Israelites labeled Elijah a troublemaker; Jeremiah was thought to be unfaithful to the state and a secret friend to the Chaldeans; the apostles were considered as intolerable disturbers who had turned the world upside down. Often the treasure is disregarded—despite its inestimable value—because of the vessel in which it comes. But when sinners are turned, this mist of prejudice is immediately scattered. Then doctrine, which before was nauseating and caused the heart to rise in opposition, will be appealing and desirable. Then a servant of Christ will be esteemed and obeyed who before was looked upon as the "offscouring" and "filth of the world" (1 Cor. 4:13).

Converts are turned from the works of darkness. These works are cast off (Rom. 13:12), and no known sin is allowed. They perceive the fruitlessness of their former ways and are ashamed of them (Rom. 6:21). Formerly they went on securely in sin because they did not know where they were going, but now they perceive that these works lead to eternal darkness. And so they are made free from sin—that is, from slavery to sin—and have become servants of righteousness. Sin may plead hard against being cast away, but all its pleas are invalid. The so-called advantageous sin pleads, "I have raised you from a low to a high degree; I have filled your wallet and put food on your table. By me you have attained your profitable position, and if it wasn't for me you would have been little better than a beggar. Will you now cast me off, having been so beneficial and advantageous?" But the convert is able to reply to such a plea. Whatever he gained unjustly he must restore, and if he had trusted in God and done good, he would have fared better. Unrighteous wealth comes with a curse, and when he thrived in wickedness, he was destitute of true riches. It is a wonder that in the midst of such dishonest and worldly gain he did not lose his soul long ago. Now, therefore, he is resolved against sinful gain for fear that he will, without noticing, lose God, Christ, and his soul.

Like the "advantageous sin," the alleged pleasurable sin is not without its arguments for being cherished: "I have pleased your flesh and made your heart happy. I made your days and nights insensibly pass away. I gratified your senses and made you sing for joy. I stupefied and silenced that vehement thing called 'conscience' when it pricked and tortured you. I chased away your cares and made you forget your sorrows. Often you thought I was delightful and embraced me as an adorable thing. Why should I now be banished and killed as if I were an enemy? Is an afflicted soul and broken heart preferable to the sweetness I am able and willing to give you?" The convert's ear is deaf to this temptation, however. The following answer is enough to dash all such appeals: the pleasures of sin are but for a season (Heb. 11:25), but the pains of hell (which are sure to follow without conversion) will never have an end and will never be mitigated. The rich man, who lived lightheartedly and extravagantly every day, begged unsuccessfully for a simple drop of water when he was cast into the flames. Thus, the works of darkness are cast off by the convert; the pleasure and gain of these evil works is nothing compared to the pain and loss that will speedily follow.

Conversion: Turning to Light

Second, as conversion involves turning from darkness, so also it includes being turned to light. Ephesians 5:8 states, "For ye were sometimes darkness, but now are ye light in the Lord: walk as children of light." Also, 2 Corinthians 4:6 records, "For God, who commanded the light to shine out of darkness, hath shined in our hearts, to give the light of the knowledge of the glory of God in the face of Jesus Christ." This light has three facets: to reveal, direct, and operate.

First, this light reveals. The apostle Paul tells us, "Whatsoever doth make manifest is light" (Eph. 5:13). The convert sees what he never saw before. There may be many toads, serpents, and other loathsome and disgusting creatures in a dungeon, but until the light shines he cannot see these creatures. Light, when it breaks in, reveals them. And so many impure and offensive lusts reside in a man's heart, but he does not acknowledge or dislike them until the light reveals them. The convert sees his sin and shame. He is sensible of the diseases within his own heart and the absolute necessity of a cure. His interest also is revealed to him: to seek first the kingdom of God and His righteousness, to secure his soul (which is of far greater value than the world), and to care about "the one thing [that] is needful...that good part, which shall not be taken away" (Luke 10:42).

Second, this light directs. It guides those who travel along the pathway of peace and truth. The lamp of the Word (the Spirit joining with and teaching by it) shows which paths are perverse and crooked in order that they may be avoided. It also directs and leads to the ways that are pleasing to God and pleasant in themselves; these ways are so exceedingly safe that no one who continued to walk in them ever missed heaven. We are directed to believe and obey, and, where faith and obedience are linked together, the sure fruit of this union will be glory, honor, and immortality.

Third, this light operates in a powerful manner, and heat accompanies it. Converts were told before of the evil and folly of sin, but now they see this more clearly by another light, and their hearts are warmed with indignation against sin. They are deeply affected by sin, sorrowing because of it and abhorring it. Before, they were informed of the mercy, all-sufficiency, and numerous other perfections of God, but now they have such a view of His glory in the face of Christ that it kindles the fire of love, and this love urges them to labor. When Caleb saw the Promised Land, he was very eager to rise at once and possess it (Num. 13:30). Similarly, when this light shines and reveals the celestial Canaan and directs converts how to get there, how great will be the watching, praying, resisting, striving, and storming!

Conversion: Turning from the Power of Satan

Third, conversion implies being turned from the power of Satan. He is the spirit that works and rules in the "children of disobedience" (Eph. 2:2), possessing them until they are converted. But upon conversion he is cast out, and his strongholds are thrown down. Considering the devil's hatred, power, and subtlety, what a merciful thing it is to have broken the cords with which he led us captive! We understand three things about being turned from the power of Satan; we will discuss these briefly.

Those who are converted are freed from Satan's dominion. They have wisdom and grace to resist his usurped authority. Those who are not under the law but under grace enjoy the promise that sin will not have dominion over them (Rom. 6:14). This necessarily implies that Satan's dominion over them is destroyed, for it is by the power of sin that he holds it. The net is now broken and the soul escapes like a bird freed from a trap. The unconverted sinner is a slave to Satan; if the devil tells him to go, he goes—even runs—although it is to his own ruin. The devil simply has to ask, and the sinner fulfills his desire. The sinner freely gives up his time, his body, and even his soul upon Satan's request. But the convert draws near to God and is strengthened by the grace of God so that, instead of being commanded by Satan, he orders Satan to flee from him.

Those who are converted cease from Satan's work. They know how corrupt and injurious, both to God and their own souls, the devil's business is. And they know there is a better work than his, namely, the work of the Lord which they are happy to labor in; they can never abound too much in this work.

Satan's baits become despicable to those who are converted. It is through this bait that the devil is so powerful. The god of this world makes great use of its sinful pleasures to entice and ensnare the children of men. He exaggerates sensual delights, luxurious living, costly possessions, reputation among men, and pleasant recreations. He suggests, "How happy these will make you!" He tells sinners of the worth of silver and gold and endeavors to set their hearts on fire by its vain beauty and appeal. But the convert, by the eye of faith, looks higher than these things. He sees the vanity of the creature. He knows what displeases God, and so, to him, the world appears as an empty bubble, insignificant and empty. His wounded conscience cannot not be cured by anything the world could offer.[1] The convert is made to look upward, and there he perceives more durable riches, more lasting pleasure than the world can brag of. And so he is not impressed or enticed with the things that are seen, but longs for the things that are not seen. Though he is in the world, yet he looks beyond it. He is like Moses who, having "respect unto the recompense of the reward," refused to be called the son of Pharaoh's

---

1. Latin: *Nullis medicabilis herbis.*

daughter and slighted the pleasures of sin and all the treasures of Egypt (Heb. 11:26).

Conversion: Turning to God

Fourth, as conversion involves turning from the power of Satan, it also implies being turned to God. Scripture declares, "Turn ye unto me, saith the LORD of hosts, and I will turn unto you" (Zech. 1:3). Many who come to a king's palace busy themselves by examining the curious wall hangings and pictures, but the wise statesman does not pay attention to these things. His business is with the king himself. Similarly, while most of creation is busy with admiring and pursuing this, that, and the other vanity, the convert (who hereby shows himself to be truly wise) approaches and focuses on God who made all things; it is God who can make him far happier than vanities are able to do.

When the sinner turns to God, he looks to Him in terms of a threefold relation: as his Lord, as his Father, and as his ultimate end. We will address each of these in turn. First, the convert eyes God as a Lord. He bows to His sovereignty and submits himself to His scepter. Other lords in the past had dominion over him (Isa. 26:13), but now his resolution is fixed and absolute to confess no Lord but God alone. The convert stoops to and complies with the will of God. If the convert is informed that God is displeased with his natural and passionate inclinations, it is enough to stop the current of his desires. The testimonies of the Lord are the rule whereby the convert orders his conduct, and when he hears that God commands him to keep His precepts diligently, his heart immediately echoes back, "O that my ways were directed to keep thy statutes!" (Ps. 119:5). He dares not presumptuously commit the evil the Word forbids or omit the good the Word commands.

Certainly there will be failings and infirmities. James says, "In many things we offend all," but this evil is a burden to the convert. In contrast, the convert approves and consents to the law of God and delights in it as holy, just, and good. The convert does not wish that the law were less holy and that it would allow him liberty to sin, but he wishes that his heart and life were more holy and that his life would be made more and more conformable to the law (which distinguishes him from a hypocrite).

The convert eyes God as his Father, or as willing to become his Father in Jesus Christ. It was truly said by one of the ancients, "None such a Father as God, none so full of fatherly affections."[2] God is able to meet the needs of every returning prodigal, and He is far more willing to impart His grace on those who see their need and ask for it than earthly parents are when giving bread to their hungry children (Matt. 7:11). This is great

---

2. Latin: *Tam Pater nemo, tam puis* [sic] *nemo.* The quotation is from Tertullian.

encouragement to returning to God. Jesus gave the parables of the lost sheep, lost coin, and lost son primarily to encourage sinners to come home to God (Luke 15). The man rejoiced when he found his sheep, as did the woman when she recovered her piece of silver. Though necessity drove the lost child home (he was ready to perish), and though he came home in rags, having foolishly wasted his inheritance, his kind father, as soon as he saw his son, ran to him, had compassion on him, embraced him, kissed him, clothed him, adorned him, and made a great feast for him. He was overjoyed that the lost child was found, that his dead son was alive again.

Surely we may conclude that God is willing to receive those who, sensible of their sin and unprofitable perversion of everything right (Job 33:27), return to Him with their whole heart. It is true that the convert's sins and unbelieving heart together fill him many times with doubts and fears. He remembers God and is troubled because he has so bitterly provoked Him. He is afraid to call Him Father, and very much doubts that he will be received. But faith and hope are encouraged by such promises as found in 2 Corinthians 6:17–18: "Touch not the unclean thing; and I will receive you, and will be a Father unto you, and ye shall be my sons and daughters, saith the Lord Almighty."

In turning to God, the convert also sees God as his ultimate end. In other words, glorifying God and enjoying Him is his purpose in turning to God. While unconverted he knew he lived in a way that dishonored the giver of life, the One who controls every person's breath. But now he zealously desires to walk worthy of the Lord, to please Him in all things and be fruitful in those works that are to His praise. Before turning to God he pursued self and his own sinful desires; his highest aim was to gratify his worldly and fleshly inclinations with things that his carnal and corrupted mind judged to be suitable. He did not care if he injured and provoked the Lord. But now he is of another mind. His purpose like that of the angels and of Christ: to honor and please the God of glory. And not only is this his aim in his spiritual actions, but also in his civil and natural actions and in his recreations (which hereby become spiritualized). He takes Paul's words in 1 Corinthians 10:31 seriously: "Whether therefore ye eat, or drink, or whatsoever ye do, do all to the glory of God." Now he lives like God's creature, like His son, whereas before he lived only to himself.

By thus glorifying God, the convert is rightly able to enjoy Him. He looks upon God as the best portion and therefore fixes himself firmly upon Him. He thinks, "Let the men of the world take the things of the world if they please. Let them pursue empty bubbles. Let them strain and work for that which, when attained, will only produce further exasperation. My soul seeks after God. He alone deserves my pursuit. He alone, when found, can completely satisfy me."

Nothing short of God will content the convert. Wealth, reputation, and sensual delights cannot do it. Even the sacraments are like empty breasts and broken cisterns unless he enjoys communion with God in them. The convert prays for God, listens for God, fasts for God, and comes to the Lord's Table for God. Earth is like hell when God is absent, and the convert judges that heaven would not be heaven if God were not always present. In summary, conversion lies in being turned from darkness to light and turning from the power of Satan to God.

Jesus Christ: The Mediator whereby We Alone Can Turn to God

I must briefly address through whom it is that sinners must turn to God if they would be received. The truth is simple: it is through Christ alone. Paul plainly affirms that it is through Christ that both Jews and Gentiles have access by one Spirit to the Father (Eph. 2:18). And our Lord clearly says in John 14:6, "I am the way, the truth, and the life: no man cometh unto the Father, but by me." It is impossible that such guilty and polluted creatures, such as we have made ourselves by sin, should ever be accepted before a just and holy God without a mediator. Thus, it follows that we must look to Jesus, to use the apostle's phrase, in whom God is reconciling the world to Himself (2 Cor. 5:19). Were it not for Jesus the

Mediator, we would not dare approach God, but would fly away for fear of being consumed as we deserve.

Now when we look to Jesus the Mediator, we must look on Him as our righteousness, as our advocate, and as our helper. First, we must look on Christ as our righteousness. This is the name of the branch that was to spring from David, who was to be called "THE LORD OUR RIGHTEOUSNESS" (Jer. 23:6). No one may come to God without righteousness. Our own righteousness is like filthy rags, and because it is rags it is not able to cover us; because it is like *filthy* rags it cannot adorn or commend us (Isa. 64:6). Therefore, we must look unto Jesus' righteousness so that, because of His obedience and suffering in our stead, our sins may be forgiven and our persons accepted in God's sight. Christ's righteousness imputed to believers is perfect and sufficient; the pure and piercing eye of God cannot detect the least flaw in it. If we are covered with this righteousness, none of our sins will appear against or convict us. Christ has died and, upon His death, God justifies. Who, therefore, will accuse or condemn those who believe?

We must also look upon Christ as our advocate. First John 2:1 states, "If any man sin, we have an advocate with the Father, Jesus Christ the righteous." This advocate suffered to purchase pardon and grace; moreover, He intercedes that these gifts may be given to returning sinners. Certainly, God, His Father, always hears Him. We should consider—and be encouraged by—what a great high priest we have at the right hand of God. When the sinner looks at his broken self and petitions for remission of sin, for the healing of his spiritual disease, and for the salvation of his hell-bound soul, this advocate will take the sinner's petition and present it to His Father. This request will be granted. Indeed, the answer will be infinitely more than the sinner can desire or conceive.

Finally, we must look upon Christ as our helper. He strengthens weak knees; without Him we would not be able to take one step in the way to life. The Lord Jesus is aptly called "the author and finisher of our faith" (Heb. 12:2), for it is by Him that believers are said to have access to that grace wherein they stand (Rom. 5:2). The sinner must be made aware of his own insufficiency to turn himself, to set himself at liberty, so that he may look to the Son of God to bring his soul out of prison, set him free from the curse of the law and the bondage of corruption, and enable him to come and cling to God.

CHAPTER 5

Concluding Applications

Since God calls sinners again and again to turn, it is extremely important for everyone to examine whether this call has been obeyed. It is wise to test our faith against the standard of God's Word, for there is much counterfeit Christianity in the world. It is easy and common to be mistaken in this matter, but there is no mistake more dangerous; if persisted in, it will not be long before it is impossible to correct mistakes about salvation. The damned know they have deceived themselves, but it is too late to think of turning back. The door to mercy is shut and barred and will be barred forever. Theodoret, commenting upon Ezekiel 33:11, observed that the doubling of the words "turn ye, turn ye," underscores the sincerity that is required in conversion. An empty and outward show only sets us further from God.

On Being "Almost Converted"

Some changes appear to be evidences of conversion, but in the end fall short both of grace and glory. People cannot be said to be converted who are turned only to smaller matters and opinions in religion. Suppose your opinion is orthodox and right. What benefit is that if your heart is not right in the sight of God? Some pride themselves because they have the name of "nonconformists," but what does it signify unless they refuse to conform to the sinful fashions and customs of the world? On the other hand, those who boast of being called "sons of the church" have no advantage if their swearing, lying, and hatred of holiness shows them to be sons of the devil.

People are not converted if their turning is only partial. Saul partly obeyed the command of the Lord concerning Amalek; Saul utterly destroyed the vile and worthless things, but he spared delicate Agag and the best of the spoil (1 Sam. 15:9). This partial obedience is counted as great rebellion in verse 23. Many will yield to God's call in some degree: they will consent to kill the sins they can easily spare, but they will not touch the chief and dearest sin. Herod was a partial convert. In many ways he obeyed John the Baptist's preaching, but when John commanded him to turn from his incest with Herodias, Herod would not listen. Instead of obeying the message, he persecuted and later killed the messenger.

Those who turn to God only in times of extremity and afterward are guilty of revolting are not converted. When Sinai was set on fire before their eyes, Israel turned to God for fear of being consumed. They cried

out saying that they would hear and do whatever the
Lord should say to them (Deut. 5:27). But before a
few days passed, they turned out of the way that God
commanded them and fell into gross idolatry. We read:
"When [God] slew them, then they sought him: and
they returned and enquired early after God. For their
heart was not right with him, neither were they sted-
fast in his covenant" (Ps. 78:34, 37). How many sickbed
resolutions have looked like conversions but, upon the
return of health, have vanished away? True conversion, however, is a lasting change. Certainly there may
be periods of decline and slumber; as Matthew 25:5
records, even the wise virgins "slumbered and slept."
While this was not a wise choice, true converts never
go so far as to choose anything but God as their chief
happiness. Reader, beware of being "almost a convert" in
much the same way as you would not wish to be "almost
saved" and "certainly damned."

Distinguishing the True Convert from
the "Almost Converted"

But, you may ask, "How is true conversion differentiated
from all those shows whereby multitudes are deluded?"
The answer to this is in several particulars. First, in true
conversion the heart is turned from loving every known
iniquity. The strength of sin lies in the love of it, and love
of sin is plain evidence that it still possesses the heart.
Psalm 119:128 is the language of a convert: "I esteem

all thy precepts concerning all things to be right; and I hate every false way." God principally requires the convert's love. If you love sin, how can you dare say you are turned? It is not sufficient to abstain from the outward act of sin—a hypocritical Pharisee may do as much—but your very soul must abhor it. The sin that you most desired, most delighted in, will be most detested when conversion is sincere. The covetous man, when turned, will most abhor covetousness; the unclean, their filthiness; the proud, their pride. This is the case because by these treasured sins they most displeased and dishonored God, and by them they were greatly polluted and defiled.

Next, in true conversion there is a renewing of the whole man. Paul in 2 Corinthians 5 says that *all things* are new in those who are new creatures and that the old things are passed away. Thus, the *whole* man is sanctified, although he is not wholly sanctified. In other words, every part is changed, though the change is not perfect or completed. In the true convert his understanding is enlightened, his conscience is made tender and has a great influence, his heart desires God along with His favor and fellowship, and he offers his bodily members as instruments of righteousness unto holiness. The convert willingly resigns and gives up his entire self, body and spirit, to the Lord.

Third, true converts desire to be turned more and more; they hunger after a greater degree of righteousness. The remaining desires of the flesh are a burden, and the Spirit strives against them (Gal. 5:17). The convert looks to God to perfect what He has already worked in him; the convert prays, "Lord, Thou hast done much for me, but there is much more still to do. There are many enemies still to slay, many diseases still to heal, many spots still to wash out, and many wrinkles still to smooth. Oh, Thou who hast laid the foundation, raise up the entire building and at last put in place the top stone, that I may cry, 'Grace, grace, forever!'"

Fourth, in true conversion there is a pure and fervent love for others who have turned to God. Love for the brethren is a sign of being passed from death to life (1 John 3:14). However lowly, poor, weak, and despised by the world they may be, yet if they are saints they will be esteemed and owned as brothers by the true convert. Our love is right when the more holy someone is, the more we love him and the more holy are his wishes for us. We love him more ardently even when he plainly addresses the sin he sees in us. We can rejoice in his grace, even if it is somewhat obscured.

Lastly, in true conversion there is a pity toward the unconverted. Those who are turned have escaped danger, and they cannot help but be moved at the thought of another's peril. How can they not mourn over their relations and acquaintances who are without Christ in the world? They are on a hazardous course. When they go to sleep, it is possible that they will wake up in the midst of unquenchable flames. When they leave their houses, they may be in hell before they return. They hang over the bottomless pit by the small thread of their lives, and a thousand things may happen every day that are sufficient to snap that thread. Then into hell they would fall, without any hope of redemption. Oh, what a sad state is that of the ungodly! If you who are wives should wake in the night and find your husband dead by your side, would it not exceedingly grieve you? Or if you who are fathers should suddenly find your children dead before your eyes, would not your heart be extremely affected? And surely if your husband, wife, or children are dead in sins, in danger of being damned forever, you have much more reason to be concerned for them and to endeavor by advice, prayers, and tears to see them turned and reconciled to God.

Now, reader, examine yourself by these evidences of conversion. If you find them in yourself you may rejoice, for these plainly show that your name is written in the Book of Life. But if you love any sin, your mind, conscience, heart, and life are all defiled. And if unchanged, you do not desire renewing grace. If you delight in carnal things and hate God's saints, this demonstrates that you are a stranger to conversion and are presently in a very bitter condition.

A Word of Warning to the Unconverted

Irrespective of who you are—high or low, rich or poor, male or female—if you read this book and have never turned, I am sent to you from God with heavy tidings. This message should—unless you have lost all sensibility—cause you to be like Belshazzar; upon seeing the handwriting on the wall, his "countenance was changed, and his thoughts troubled him, so that the joints of his loins were loosed, and his knees smote one against another" (Dan. 5:6). I do not prophesy good concerning you, but evil. I have a message to deliver to you, but it is one of lamentation, murmuring, and woe. You are, perhaps, fun-loving and secure, but this is like a sick and insane man's laughter: the laughter is only further evidence that the man's condition is severe. Sinner, you do not have reason to smile while in your natural state. You have many threats levied against you. Suppose that you were surrounded with guns pointed at you, all ready to be fired at once. This would be nothing compared to the dreadful threats and curses the just and jealous God has uttered against the sinner. Open your eyes and look around you. You should see enough that would greatly terrify you: above there is an angry God; below, a flaming hell; behind, an innumerable host of sins pursue you; and before you, Satan and the world lead you along the broad way to destruction.

More particularly, however, several truths should be impressed upon your heart if you are unconverted. While unconverted, you are also unpardoned. You stand indebted for many thousands of talents, and not even one cent's worth of all that debt is paid. If the smallest transgression makes you liable to the curse of the law, imagine what an accursed wretch your many and mighty sins have made you. If you return to God and acknowledge your iniquity, He has promised to do away with all your sin; He will lay the load on the back of Jesus the Mediator. But, if you will not turn, you alone must bear it. Sin is not what you imagine it to be. Think of Adam's first transgression in eating the forbidden fruit and how hurtful it was. Adam believed the serpent, and his sin was aggravated because he would have been as God; but he made God out as a liar, and, indeed, rejected the whole covenant of life. Not only did his sin affect himself, but every one of his descendants suffers because of it. And if one sin has brought a curse upon all people, how will you be able to stand under all the sins you have committed? Sin makes the whole creation groan; it causes the damned to lament and despair, and it will be an intolerable load to them forever. Our Lord also found sin to be very heavy; it caused Him great anguish and made His soul exceedingly sorrowful, even unto death. Indeed, God Himself complains that He is pressed with iniquity much like a cart that is pressed full of sheaves (Amos 2:13). Given the severity of sin, will you, sinner, make light of it? Oh, how heavy will you one day feel it!

You must also consider that while unconverted you are storing up for yourself more and more wrath, all of which will break loose on the great day of wrath. Your score is large already, but every day you increase the tally more. Every day you make new wounds, though your conscience now is so dull that it feels nothing. As your sin increases, so do the vials of divine indignation, one day to be emptied upon your head. It is unnatural and cruel to be a devil to yourself, to be your own soul's murderer. You are continually setting yourself at a greater distance from God, provoking Him (who alone can be your refuge and salvation) to be more and more against you. You will perceive at last that you were your own enemy and acted to your own confusion. Thus, Jeremiah 7:19 records, "Do they provoke me to anger? saith the LORD: do they not provoke themselves to the confusion of their own faces?"

Consider that while unconverted you make yourself more and more unfit for glory and blessedness. The more impure you are, the more unfit you are to see God. The abominations that you produce and love make you an improper inhabitant for the New Jerusalem. The inheritance in heaven is an inheritance of saints; it is incorruptible and undefiled (1 Peter 1:4). Every resident of heaven is holy, and so too are their actions. There is not a vain or sinful word spoken there nor an impure desire or thought. What then would you do there among this holy company unless a change is worked in you?

If you do not turn, you will certainly die. Life is as far off as death is near. The psalmist tells us, "God is angry with the wicked every day. If he turn not, he will whet his sword; he hath bent his bow, and made it ready" (Ps. 7:11–12). When the instruments of death are prepared, this is a sign that God will make quick work of the offender and suddenly cut him off. Death is aptly called a "king of terrors" with respect to the sinner's death. Upon death the ungodly have already received all their good things, and then they will only experience eternal evil. Their torments begin at death, and this will never end. As long as God is God, they will have Him for their enemy. As long as God is happy, they will lie in the most extreme misery. No tongue can utter or heart imagine the horror of this. An angry, sin-revenging Lord will lay your heavy load upon you, and yet will keep you from sinking into nothing. He will uphold your being in order that you are plagued forever. He will show His mighty power in holding you up with one hand and eternally lashing you with the other.

A Word of Consolation to the Convert

You who have obeyed the call of God to turn, I am also commanded to speak peace and comfort to you: "Comfort ye, comfort ye my people, saith your God" (Isa. 40:1). The unconverted are not more cursed than you are blessed. I have several things to tell you that will make your heart leap for joy. First, God has had thoughts of love toward you from before the foundation of the world. He predestinated and chose you unto the adoption of children long before you existed (Ephesians 1). From eternity He designed to make you heirs, even joint heirs with Christ, to that kingdom and glory that cannot be compared to the sufferings of this present age. And since the love of God toward you is from everlasting and is coeternal with Himself, it can never in time be changed.

Second, God has justified you freely by His grace through the redemption of Jesus Christ (Rom. 3:24). Psalm 103:12 declares, "As far as the east is from the west, so far hath he removed our transgressions from us." And surely that's as far as you can desire. They are cast into the depth of the sea. This means when looked for, they will not be found, just as we despair that those things cast into the bottom of the ocean will never be recovered. Christ was wounded for your transgressions and bruised for your iniquities (Isa. 53:5). And as the imputation of your sins to Christ caused Him to undergo real suffering, so the imputation of His righteousness to you will cause a real exemption from that wrath and punishment you justly deserve. Be of good cheer, converts, your sins are forgiven, and, consequently, the curse of affliction and the sting of death are taken away.

Third, it won't be long before you as a convert are glorified. Romans 8:30 says: "Moreover whom he did predestinate, them he also called: and whom he called, them he also justified: and whom he justified, them he also glorified." The Lord has promised that those who overcome will sit with Him on His throne. But not only will you overcome, you will be more than conquerors through Him who loved you. Mansions are already prepared for you, and, when you are prepared for those mansions, you will be ushered into them. Then neither the fury nor the favor of the world will be a temptation. Satan's fiery darts will not be able to reach you when you have entered into the third heaven. When you come to the entrance of the New Jerusalem, you will shake hands with both sin and misery at the door, and neither of them will be able to follow. Tears will be wiped away, and the cause of sorrow will be gone. No cloud will obscure your clear view of God; the Sun of Righteousness will shine forever without any eclipse. You will experience entire joy without grief, perfect peace without any trouble, complete holiness without the least remainder of corruption, and full blessedness without end.

A Word of Exhortation to Turn to God

Who would not now wish to become a convert? Do you have anything to say against this pardon or against this glory already spoken of? Here is the question: Do you prefer eternal pleasure or eternal torment? If only you would come to your senses, then, I am certain you would come to God immediately. In the following I make several arguments to persuade you to turn to God.

First, if you do not turn, you cannot make sense of the purpose of your existence. You must not think God gave you a being and sent you into the world to please yourselves, to satisfy your immoderate and corrupt desires, or to live carelessly and rebelliously against Him. But that is what you do until you are converted. Did the Lord give you a mind, and not intend that you should know and understand Him? Did He give you a heart to love and to desire, and not design that He be the chief object of both? Did He give you affections that you should give them away to sin and vanity? Do not mistake the purpose for which you were made any longer, lest you cause the Lord to repent and grieve that He made you (Gen. 6:6) and so resolve to destroy His own workmanship. If you continue obstinately and without understanding, "he that made [you] will not have mercy on [you], and he that formed [you] will show [you] no favour" (Isa. 27:11).

Second, unless you turn, you cannot make sense of the purpose of Christ's death and the redemption it purchased. Our Lord did not die only to expiate offenses, but also to purify unto Himself a peculiar people, zealous of good works, and that "in the body of his flesh through death, [He might present] you holy and unblameable" (Col. 1:22). Hebrews 9:14 says, "How much more shall the blood of Christ, who through the eternal Spirit offered himself without spot to God, purge your conscience from dead works to serve the living God?" From these and similar passages, it follows that not only our pardon but our purity was purposed by the Lord Jesus. But how can we be pure unless we turn to God from the sin that defiles us? Christ knows how sin sickens and debases our nature, and so He Himself was slain that sin might be killed. Will you then dare live in sin? Listen to what Peter says: "Who his own self bare our sins in his own body on the tree, that we, being dead to sins, should live unto righteousness: by whose stripes ye were healed" (1 Peter 2:24). Just as the death of Christ is an argument to persuade us to turn from sin, so, from this death, we can derive virtue and power in order to subdue sin.

Third, you are further obliged to turn to God because of His condescension in giving you permission to do so. If an impassable gulf was fixed after the first transgression, if the turning of fallen man was as impossible as the turning of fallen angels, the Lord could not have been charged as unjust. But, although you have departed from Him, He calls after you. Without harming His justice, He has found a way to show you mercy. And yet the devils were never called to conversion; as soon as they sinned, they were bound in chains of darkness that will never be loosed. But listen to what Wisdom says in Proverbs 8:4: "Unto you, O men, I call; and my voice is to the sons of man." Nevertheless, you have often plugged your ears. If only you would hear so that your soul may live. Your prolonged deafness may provoke the Lord to close His mouth, and then you will never be converted, never healed.

Fourth, consider both *who* it is that calls you to turn and *what* His design is in calling you to turn. You are a lost wretch who does not have skill, will, or power to save yourself. And He who calls you is a God who has all power and mercy; further, His purpose is to make His power and mercy known to you. His aim is to bring you near that He might show Himself to you in a way that He does not manifest Himself to the world, to shield you from danger, to supply your needs with the riches of His glory, to deliver you from every evil work, and to preserve you for His heavenly kingdom. Is there any harm in this?

Fifth, it is unreasonable that the world or sin should delay you from turning to God. You would do well to turn from sin, for it deserves your hatred. You would do well to turn your hearts from idolizing the world and the things of it, for they deserve your scorn. Everything besides God is either hurtful or helpless. Nothing is more hurtful than sin, and those who expected help from creatures have found themselves destitute and forlorn.

Sixth, if you turn to God He will not fail to turn to you. He will turn His ear and hear your cry. His hand will be on you for good, and you will be secure in His palm. He is greater than all, and no one is able to pluck you out of His hands. He will not hide, but turn His face toward you. He will give you peace as well as mercy, and He will let you know that pardon is multiplied so that your love also may be increased—the debtor who is forgiven much, loves much. Finally, He will turn His stream of benefits toward you. The Lord will do good to you and delights in doing so. You will not lack temporal things, and He will shower upon you abundant spiritual blessings. At last you will ascend and be admitted into His immediate presence where God will turn to you and never withdraw again. Do not be afraid or dismayed at those who might turn against you because of your conversion; the Lord Himself is with and for you, and He will turn to good what adversaries mean for evil.

Seventh, not only do God's Word, ministers, and Spirit call you, but also His providences call you to turn. Both His mercies and His judgments exhort you to convert to Him. The streams of goodness that continually run toward you—at times swelling and overflowing—signify that it is wise to forsake the broken cisterns and come to the fountain of living waters. His mercies tell you that it is good to return to and obtain an interest in the Father who gives them. Then these mercies will truly be given in mercy. Cords of love are wrapped around you to draw you to the God of love and peace. Oh, that you would run to Him! The riches of His goodness are unlocked and displayed that by them you may be led to repentance (Rom. 2:4).

Similarly, His judgments are inflicted with the same purpose in mind. Judgments, as it were, say: "Come, and let us return unto the LORD: for he hath torn, and he will heal us; he hath smitten, and he will bind us up"

(Hos. 6:1). The Great Fire of London of 1666, for example, called on its inhabitants, and of the whole land, to abhor themselves and repent in dust and ashes. These people not only heard of God with their ears, but saw Him with their eyes, marching out so dreadfully against them. Those many thousands who were cut off by the plague of pestilence, although they are dead, still speak; their message is, "Oh, you who are alive, return unto the Lord your God, for after death it will be too late."

Finally, consider that as of right now it is not too late to return to God. Though you have been foolish and stubborn till now, if you will awake and yield yourselves to the Lord, He will forgive; although you have shut the door to keep sin in and keep Christ out, if now at last you open as the gospel knocks, and consent that your lusts should be driven out and the Lord Jesus enter, He is ready to receive you into grace and favor; all former denials, insults, and rejections will be forgotten and forgiven. The scepter is still held forth; the Lord is not yet removed from His mercy seat. Mercy and grace may be had if you will come for them. But if you will not acknowledge this well-offered gift and are resolved to continue in your stubborn way, God may soon swear an oath in wrath that you will never enter His rest. God may say, "He that is unjust, let him be unjust still: and he which is filthy, let him be filthy still" (Rev. 22:11). "He who is joined to the profits and pleasures of the world, making these his idols, let him alone. He who despises the offer of grace will not have another, and he who now refuses to be converted will never be a convert."

Oh, that I could prevail by all these arguments. But, lest they have no impression on you, and for fear that they slip out of your mind and have no influence on your heart, I will second them with three voices of exhortation: a voice from hell, a voice from heaven, and the voice of Christ Himself.

Exhortation: A Voice from Hell

Imagine that a damned sinner has lain many years in the burning lake. Suppose he was allowed to leave and appear before us; imagine that a river of tears is gushing from his eyes, and for a while he remains expressionless. Then, after some time, he says:

"Curse the day I was born, and that night they said 'A boy is conceived!' Let that day be darkness; let not God regard it from on high, neither let light shine upon it. It would be better never to have been born at all than to be forever miserable! How intolerable is the gnawing of the never-dying worm; how hot and unquenchable are those flames that are kindled by the breath of the Lord!

"The world is extremely mistaken concerning sin. They think it light and pleasant, and I once thought so as well. But now I realize how miserably I was deceived. I feel sin's weight and taste; indeed, I am drunk with its gall and wormwood. Before I did not believe it, but it truly is a fearful thing to fall into the hands of the living God. His mighty hands have taken hold of me and bound me hand and foot and thrown me into outer darkness. And there I must lie tortured for all eternity! Oh, how this word "eternity" rends my very heart, kills all hope, sinks and overwhelms me in utter desperation.

"If after millions and millions of years my torments were to end, I would strengthen myself under my sorrows, but, after this long time has passed, I will be as far from being free as the first moment I was imprisoned. So my grief knows no bounds because misery knows none. What frenzy possessed me that, for the sake of a little and momentary pleasure offered by sin, I chose to dwell with devouring fire and inhabit everlasting burnings!

"But I must only blame myself. God is severe, but He is not in the least unrighteous. He called, but I refused. He stretched forth His hand, but I disregarded Him. I disregarded His counsel and would have nothing to do with His reproofs. I remember very well that He spoke to me often to turn off the paths that lead to destruction and misery, but I refused to listen. I was warned to flee from the wrath to come, but I would not hear. He entreated me to be reconciled, but I resolved to continue a rebel. I would not be made clean though the Lord waited to be gracious!

"What! Will any of you continue in the same desperate mind that I had? Will you still cherish the same sins that led to my ruin? See the flames about my ears.

If only you could imagine the anguish of my heart! Be wise, be wise, and accept mercy and salvation while it is offered you, for once you come to this place of torment, the Lord will forget to be gracious, and His mercy will be gone forever!"

Exhortation: A Voice from Heaven

Now imagine that one of the glorified saints who was an inhabitant of the heavenly Jerusalem, who conversed with an innumerable company of angels and saw God face to face, should, for some time, leave his blissful mansion and, with an abundance of joy and glory in his looks, utter this:

"Oh, the height, length, depth, and breadth of the love of Christ which passes knowledge! How unsearchable is His goodness, and His mercy past finding out! Worthy is the Lamb that was slain to receive power, riches, wisdom, strength, honor, glory, and blessing, for by His blood He has redeemed me, with millions more out of every race, tongue, people, and nation! I was called to turn and live, and through rich grace was enabled to obey the call. And I found out what a glorious life sincere and persevering converts are brought to. This is a life that is free from sin and suffering, a life that will never see death or be in danger of the grave.

"It is best of all to be near to God. Christ is without a doubt the best master. To be subject to Him is to reign, and reign forever! What afflicts the blind and foolish world that they see no form or attractiveness in this fairest among ten thousand, whose bright face makes heaven forget the light of the sun, moon, or stars! His beauty is all-surpassing, His grace much more than gold that perishes, and it is not lawful or possible for me to utter His glory!

"Will any of you now slight Him any longer? Open your eyes and see that you are the children of perdition, the sons of death without Him. But through Him you may be turned. Through Him you may be saved with a great and everlasting salvation. Surely, then, you have reason to value Him above all, though the whole world (or even ten thousand worlds) should stand in competition with Him."

Exhortation: Christ's Voice

Imagine, last of all, that the Lord Jesus appeared with a light brighter than the sun. Suppose some of His angels as heralds and forerunners came before Him, crying out, "Holy, holy, holy, is the Lord of Hosts," and at last Himself visibly appearing with majesty and glory. And, having struck you with awe, and having worked in you an admiration for His excellence and greatness, suppose that He said this to you:

"Look unto Me and be saved, all you ends of the earth. I am your Redeemer, and there is no one else. You have destroyed yourselves, but in Me and Me alone you may find help. Unless I make you free, sin will still reign in you; and if it reigns, it will also ruin you. Unless I bind the strong-armed man, he will keep you bound and lead you captive at his pleasure. Unless I turn and bring you near to God, you will run farther and farther away from Him until at last there is no possibility of return. How long, you ignorant souls, will you love ignorance, and you fools hate knowledge? Turn at My reproof. Behold, I will pour out My Spirit upon you. I will make My words known to you.

"I will pass by former contempt if now at last you will receive Me. I will free you from the guilt and power of sin. I will pacify My Father's anger, though by breaking His laws and despising Me, His Son, you have greatly infuriated Him. Though by nature captives, I will make you kings and priests; though by sin traitors and enemies, I will make you sons and heirs of God and coheirs with Myself, the heir of all things. You will not be miserable if all the fullness that dwells in Me can satisfy you and make you happy."

Listen to the voice of the Son of God, who is not willing that you should perish. What must I do for you to listen—after hearing these voices, will you still be fond of sin and ruin? I would even be willing that these words were my last, as long as they were powerful and effectual to convert, heal, and save all who hear them. I would be willing to expire here and be carried dead out of the pulpit upon the condition that you might hear and turn from your evil ways and live. The many thousands who have gone before me are unknown to me, but I do know that you have souls and that every soul is worth a world. I plead with you to consider your soul's interest and safety!

But lest it be in vain if I should speak only to you, I will direct my words to Him who is Lord over all:

> Would that He who irresistibly works effect a thorough and saving change in you! Oh, that He would pity those among you who are cruel unto yourselves! Oh, that He would awaken the souls that are not only asleep, but dead, and break the hearts that have made themselves an adamant stone! Oh, that He would convince you of your sin and misery and effectually turn you that you may be freed forever!

To these petitions, let every heart say amen!

A Final Word of Direction

I hope that by this time you are willing to listen to and follow some directions as to how to become sincere converts. I am confident that you would welcome and listen to directions on how to get comfort when you are in pain, directions on how to recover your health when you are sick, or some possessions you have lost. Directions from the infallible Word of truth are of far greater consequence. Therefore, consider these six final directions:

First, with a serious spirit, consider your ways. This consideration had great influence on the psalmist. Psalm 119:59–60 states: "I thought on my ways, and turned my feet unto thy testimonies. I made haste, and delayed not to keep thy commandments." That injunction is echoed in Haggai 1:5, and again in verse 7: "Thus saith the LORD of hosts; Consider your ways." Observe Ezekiel 18:14: "Now lo, if he beget a son, that seeth all his father's sins which he hath done, and considereth, and doeth not such like...." If sinners would consider the fullness of their sin when they commit evil, it would make them cease from evil and learn to do well. Consider the misery and danger of being far from God. The path you naturally walk in leads you away from Him, and Scripture says, "They that are far from thee shall perish: thou hast destroyed all them that go a whoring from thee" (Ps. 73:27). Think about these things until you find your heart so affected that you consider it to be madness to lie secure in an unconverted state. Let this thought make a deep impression: while you persist in your evil ways, you forsake the Lord and forsake your own mercies and are quickly traveling to the regions of eternal woe and darkness.

Second, study the vanity of former excuses. I know the natural man is full of them, but it is very easy to answer them. "Sin," you say, "is riveted in my very nature."

You need to cry to heaven that your nature be changed.

"But sin is the common practice."

Your danger is the greater and you should be more careful lest you are overwhelmed in the ruin that will be so general.

"But my lusts are profitable and pleasant, and why should I abandon them?"

Consider, soul, whether the damned who have lost their souls and eternal blessedness and suffer the vengeance of eternal fire have any reason to boast of gain or pleasure.

"But men will deride and scorn me if I become a convert."

Those men are beside themselves, and sober people need not be concerned at the laughter of the insane. Condemn their contempt; despise the shame they cast upon you. Shortly they themselves will wish that, instead of scorning you, they had imitated you.

"But to turn to and follow God is very hard, and the difficulty is a very great discouragement."

The work is hard indeed, but so too is the offered strength and assistance. The Lord will effect all your works in you and for you (Isa. 26:12). He commands only what He is ready to help you perform.

"But if I am a convert, I will never live a pleasant hour. My tears will be my meat and drink, and my sorrows my perpetual companions."

This is a gross mistake and an unreasonable prejudice against the ways of holiness. If godliness is so melancholy, why does Scripture tell us of a peace that passes all understanding and joys that are unspeakable and full of glory? Why is David so often singing, so often harping, if gladness and religion were inconsistent?

"Oh, but if I turn, I will be exposed to suffering."

Well, suppose you are. The sufferings of this present time are incomparable with the present grace and consolation that will attend your trials, much less with the glory that will be revealed. Study the vanity of all these excuses!

Third, save yourselves from your stubborn generation. This was the advice the apostle gave to those who were awakened and pricked in their hearts (Acts 2:40). You must leave your former sinful companions; they will be a great temptation and snare to you. Carnal company is an incarnate devil who endeavors to draw as many as he can to hell along with him. Therefore, the wisest men use words of caution as found in Proverbs 4:14–15: "Enter not into the path of the wicked, and go not in the way of evil men. Avoid it, pass not by it, turn from it, and walk away." While you are not to be miserable and uncivil toward the ungodly, do not be delightfully familiar with them. Many convictions and good resolutions have cooled and vanished due to wicked company. Do not suck in any prejudices from them against true piety, and when they presume to rant against prayer, confession, fasting, profession of faith, or the Lord's Day and censure the Lord's people, look on all this as simply the ravings of those who are spiritually distracted.

Fourth, do not despise the preaching of the Word. The ministry of the Word is ordained to work faith and to turn sinners to God. Therefore, do not let drowsiness, distraction, concerns, pleasures, lusts, or the deceitfulness of riches choke this Word and hinder it from attaining its appointed end. When Ezekiel prophesied over the dead and dry bones, they revived, and a valley of dead bones became a living army. Who can tell, while you hear the preached Word under the ministry of the gospel, suddenly you may be made alive although you were dead in trespasses. Prize and frequent powerful preaching. Certainly the Word has a converting power when it is applied. Psalm 19:7 records: "The law of the LORD is perfect, converting the soul: the testimony of the LORD is sure, making wise the simple."

Fifth, do not quench the Spirit (1 Thess. 5:19). You must not stifle His conviction but improve on it. The Spirit of the Lord sometimes approaches very near to a drunkard, swearer, covetous, or unclean person and tells him that there is but a step between him and death, between him and damnation. Therefore it moves him to humiliation and to reformation. He informs him that he had better leave his sins rather than face certain judgment because of them. Such conviction may result in true conversion if they were but closed with and improved on, but thousands resist the Holy Spirit. They would rather be left alone and permitted to sin than to have the waters stirred up, even though upon stepping in they might be healed, whatever their spiritual disease. Is the Holy Spirit near you? Pay attention to His persuasions. Submit to His leadings, and beg that He not stop at common or general operations, but that He will perform a saving work in you.

Finally, lay hold on and plead the Lord's own covenant. In this covenant He has promised to give you a new heart, to cleanse you from your filthiness and idols, to put His Spirit within you, and to cause you to walk in His commandments (Ezek. 36:25–27). In other words, He has promised to convert you. Be earnest that these promises are accomplished in you. Resolve that you will not take no for an answer. The Lord will be pleased with your persistence; it will serve His own honor to grant you your request. You cannot turn yourself, but He can just as easily do this work as not do it. One word of life and power will raise you. And since He says, "Turn ye, turn ye from your evil ways; for why will ye die, O house of Israel?" then make this text into your prayer: "Turn me, turn me from my evil ways, for why should I die, O God of Israel?"